THE PSYCHOTHERAPY MANUAL
TREATMENT MODELS AND CLINICAL CASES

Phil Feldman, PhD

Bond Press

PROFESSIONALS' COMMENTS ABOUT THIS MANUAL

Jagdish Dang, MD
Medical Director, Barnert Hospital, Psychiatry Department

"Dr. Feldman's manual is an excellent and concise overview of Psychotherapy Treatment Models and Clinical Techniques. Case examples illustrate numerous effective and creative interventions. I highly recommend this manual as required reading for Mental Health Professionals who want to expand their knowledge base and gain clarity about critical psychotherapy topics. It is also well written and enjoyable to read. I plan to read it again and share it with my staff.

Mari Lou Parkinson, MSW, LSW
Passaic County Director - Family Intervention Services, NJ

"The Psychotherapy Manual - Treatment Models and Clinical Cases" is an informative resource with practical guidance for professionals involved in the helping profession. The text should be required reading for students pursuing a degree in social work or a related discipline."

Albert Wallin, CSW, CDA, CDC
Substance Abuse Specialist, St.Mary's Hospital, Passaic

" I was very impressed with Dr. Feldman's Psychotherapy Manual. My colleagues and I find it very useful in our psychiatric work."

About the Author

Dr. Phil Feldman is currently the Coordinator of the Adult Unit at the Barnert Hospital Counseling Center in New Jersey. He has been doing clinical work with adults and couples for the past 15 years. He is also an Adjunct Professor at Rutgers University, Graduate School of Social Work. Dr. Feldman works as a Clinical Training Consultant to various agencies and hospitals in New York and New Jersey. He presents on a wide range of mental health topics which include Personality Disorders, Shame and Anger, and Psychotherapy Strategies.

In addition to the "Psychotherapy Manual," Dr. Feldman is the author of "Shame Affect: Theory, Research and Clinical Treatment." The Shame manual helps sensitize practitioners about the commonality of shame affect and what strategies to use during treatment. He has also published a number of articles in professional journals on clinical topics.

As a psychotherapist, Dr. Feldman uses an eclectic approach as he works with various presenting problems. He has training in psychodynamic treatment, family therapy and cognitive behavioral therapy.

Dr. Feldman is available to provide seminars for clinical staff and can be reached at 973-977-6120.

Dedication

This manual is dedicated to my family. Your encouragement and support are the backbone of my work.

In Appreciation

I offer special thanks to my colleagues at Barnert Hospital and Professors at Rutgers University and Ackerman Institute who have discussed and explored with me various cases and clinical strategies. Their insights and wisdom have helped me develop my own approach to clinical practice.

Table of Contents

Introduction

It is my goal to present a review of the major Treatment Models and to highlight ways to integrate their perspectives into clinical practice. I will assume that readers have some familiarity with the theories and models. It is important to point out that a theory is, in essence, an explanation. It helps us understand and predict to some degree human behavior. This also includes a prediction of how emotions, cognitions, behavior and interpersonal interactions are linked. Each theory has strength and weakness. We do not have any theory that is the final word on human behavior and functioning. It is interesting to note that most clinicians conceptualize their cases and use clinical techniques based on a number of theories. Many of these therapists are unaware that they do so. Using a variety of strategies and approaches is called Eclectic Practice. This manual will take a close look at this fascinating topic and explore creative ways to work with a range of presenting problems.

It is my belief that clinicians need to develop their skills and knowledge base so that they can pull from a range of sources in order to treat their clients successfully. An old term called the "professional use of self" sums up this idea. Therapists need to be cognizant of how they interact with their clients. They should carefully choose the role they will use when starting their sessions. Will they be sympathetic, confrontational, or acting as a guide? Will they switch gears in mid session and change from confronting their

patient to a more supportive stance? These are important issues that we need to keep in mind.

The Psychotherapeutic Relationship

One of the most important components of the therapeutic relationship is trust and respect. The client needs to feel that they are in a safe environment where they can fully explore their emotional and cognitive reactions to past and current issues. Many clients feel ambivalent about attending treatment and the therapist needs to carefully address their feelings and level of motivation. Are they anxious or feeling a sense of shame as they reveal their personal problems? Do they feel coerced to come in by a third party (parole, employer, wife, etc.)? I suggest you ask the patient: "What thoughts did you have about not coming here today?" This is open ended and gives them a chance to explore their feelings about starting the therapy process. Another question to ask: "How did you manage to overcome your initial anxiety, fear, embarrassment?" This helps build rapport with them. After this exploration it is important to add: "I give you a lot of credit for pushing yourself to come in today. Most people have similar feelings when they begin." This interchange will make your client feel understood which is one of the core ingredients in successful clinical work. I believe this short discussion will also improve the chances that the client will continue treatment and feel that they are working with someone who comprehends the difficulty of starting therapy. Furthermore, clinicians should ask again after every few sessions how the client feels about attending as well as how they

feel about your relationship. This could be the most critical part of early sessions.

As the intake proceeds the therapist needs to ask a wide range of questions relating to the presenting problem, history of psychiatric treatment, medical problems, substance abuse, family makeup, legal issues, work history and any previous childhood abuse. Speaking with a respectful and caring tone of voice is essential at this stage. Any questions about childhood abuse need to be brief since the therapeutic relationship has not been firmly established. If the patient feels forced to reveal too much they may feel shameful, confused and angry. They may also decide to terminate treatment due to the forced nature of the first session. I like to begin the first session by asking easy and concrete questions so the client can settle in and get used to my voice. These include questions about their birth date, address and their experience traveling to the clinic.

During the intake, the clinician also needs to direct the session so that the client doesn't go off on tangents which are irrelevant to their goals in treatment. There is a delicate balance between allowing the patient to openly express themselves and the therapist's role of directing the process. Many neophytes in the mental health field have overextended intake sessions because they have not maintained control of the session. This is a skill that needs to be learned quickly. An essential question to be thinking about is: What is the most important thing the patient is trying to tell you?

The therapist should also monitor their speech and body language. Are you lecturing or admonishing the client? Are you constantly confronting them? Confrontation certainly has its place but should be mixed with a caring tone and supportive stance. Anyone who uses confrontation as their main approach to treatment is missing many important skills. We need to be more selective when doing treatment. The therapist needs to use critical thinking and intuition when deciding how to communicate. Typically we will be softer with a patient who has emotional problems and more firm with antisocial or aggressive patients. This is based on natural intuition. But at times the antisocial client needs emotional support and the depressed client needs to be confronted about their passivity.

An interesting area of concern is how much to reveal about oneself. One of the possible reasons to disclose about oneself is to make it easier for the patient to open up about themselves. Many clients do report that it helps them feel comfortable and a sense of trust. However do we sidetrack the therapy by revealing information? Will the patient begin to wonder about our family makeup, our relationships, or our vacation plans when we reveal some personal information? It is important to consider when it may be therapeutic to disclose personal issues. As an example when working with a couple with marital problems it can be helpful to reveal that you are married for ten years so that they feel you have an understanding about relationships and some success in marriage. In the same way, if you are working with parents and discussing their

parenting problems, you can reveal that you have raised two children for the past eight years. In some cases, the therapist may disclose they also have a chronic medical problem which they have had to accept. In most cases, the client's reaction to the therapist's disclosure will be positive. They will feel less isolated with their problem and view the therapist as having some expertise about the issue.

Excessive self disclosure can be problematic. It takes the focus off the patient. Always remember: whose session is it? The therapist should also analyze what is happening in the sessions. Are they spending time ventilating their own reactions and feelings about their life? After revealing personal information make sure to quickly refocus on the patient's problems. One of the critical goals in treatment is to communicate with warmth, genuineness, and human qualities without diminishing your authority and expertise. In essence, this is a balance between being somewhat open about oneself, yet remembering your professional role.

During the process of developing the therapeutic alliance it is worthwhile to evaluate oneself in terms of relationships. Do we have good relationships with people in our lives? Have we been successful maintaining long term relationships? How does our relationship with our spouse, family, supervisor, coworkers, and neighbors affect our connection with clients? How do we feel about the clinic, school, or hospital that we are working in? Do we feel mistreated, appreciated, and/or a sense of loyalty. If we find any of

these relationships weak what can we do to improve them? Perhaps we need therapy to work on these issues.

Clients will certainly invoke feelings within the therapist as treatment begins and progresses. You may feel: **Anger** when the patient answers their cell phone in session and begins chatting about irrelevant issues with a friend. **Disgust** when the antisocial client brags about how they steal or hurt others. **Hopeless** when the patient doesn't show any effort to change. **Anxiety** when the client questions the value of treatment. **Fear** when they describe their depression and loneliness due to divorce. **Frustration** when they do the opposite of what they planned to do since last session. Over time, the therapist will learn to cope with their reactions. With the help of a good supervisor they can explore these reactions and use them to identify how the patient impacts on others in their lives. With practice, the clinician can describe to the client how they make them feel and help them realize their impact on others. In addition, your reaction to them may help you make a diagnosis. This may take place as you conduct an intake with a Borderline patient who makes you feel anxious, manipulated and angry.

Maintaining a professional stance and monitoring one's emotions will lead to success in clinical work. As an example a 45 year old female patient with a long history of depression came for treatment. Her personality was usually easy going and kind. During one session, about 2 months after her mother died, she responded to my question about exercise saying, "I just told you I went walking

two times last week, aren't you listening?" This was out of character for her. I began to feel angry but controlled myself and said, "Have you been feeling angry lately?" She responded, "Yes, because my mother is gone and my father is already talking about getting married again. It's disrespectful to my mother." This led to an open discussion about her feelings and reactions and how to cope with her loss. Fortunately I was able to maintain an objective stance and did not become angry or defensive when she initially became aggressive. It is important to question what the meaning of the patient's statements is. Based on their communication can you feel their confusion, fear, anger, emptiness, shame, or guilt?

Another area of concern is how the clinician impacts on the client. Do we do anything that is potentially threatening to them? For example are we pushing them too hard to reveal their history of childhood abuse? Is this pushing them away? Are we questioning too aggressively about their past mistakes and making treatment into a confession. Do we relate to them as a Psychotic patient or as a unique individual? Do we have a sense that they feel treated differently than your other patients? Are we giving them extra therapy time or shortening the sessions? Have we changed the frequency of sessions based on our feelings towards them? These are key questions that need to be addressed honestly.

Furthermore the psychotherapist has a special role and is viewed as having particular insight, wisdom and authority. This perspective has a positive impact on the therapeutic process. The

parameters of treatment also help keep the client - therapist relationship well defined. Meetings take place in a professional setting (school, clinic, hospital, nursing home) and patients generally understand that it is a goal oriented meeting, rather than a casual visit. Most patients also comprehend that it is inappropriate to request a session at a restaurant, movie, amusement park, etc.

These parameters, as well as a sense of confidentiality, create an atmosphere where the client can feel safe to explore intimate topics which are too risky to discuss in more informal relationships. The clinician's task is to strike a balance: maintaining their professional role, yet communicating in a warm and spontaneous manner. As they begin this process they need to be cognizant of their goal to create a strong therapeutic relationship with the patient. The patient should feel they are being treated as a unique individual by a compassionate professional. The therapist's later goals will be to offer emotional support, help the client clarify and describe their emotional or psychological problems, and explore ways to cope.

As the relationship develops and sessions continue, the clinician will begin to recognize various strengths and weaknesses within the client. What will be your focus? The psychodynamic approach and the medical model suggest identifying the patient's pathology. The ego psychology and functional model focus on patient's strengths. Should the intrapsychic weaknesses be the main focus? Perhaps the family pathology is more important (the enmeshed family vs. the distanced family). Lastly, the patient – therapist relationship may be

of most importance. Perhaps we need to integrate these perspectives and make a multidimensional assessment of the client.

Is the patient ready for therapy? The patient needs some faith and hope that they can change and that the clinician has the ability to help them in this process (Safran and Muran, 2000). Many clients start treatment feeling demoralized and have little faith that anyone can help them. They present as bitter, cynical and depressed. Certainly these clients create strong counter-transference reactions in the therapist. This includes anxiety, fear, boredom, avoidance and wanting to transfer the case. What interventions can be used? Encourage the client to express their feelings of anger, frustration, depression and hopelessness. Help the client feel less isolated and allow them to experience their emotional problems within the context of the therapeutic relationship. As you offer warmth, support, acceptance and respect for them you fulfill some of their emotional needs. This will help them feel less isolated and will often improve their emotional turmoil. This may also serve as a model for them to connect to others in their community.

Does the patient feel accepted by the therapist? One of the dilemmas in treatment is that the therapist is pushing the client to change and does not accept the client as they are. The goal should be to create an atmosphere where the patient feels respected by the clinician and trusts them. In this way they can clarify the unacceptable parts of themselves and begin the process of change. If the therapist joins them to focus and work on these

change goals then they can collaborate effectively. It is critical to communicate that you do accept the client where they are currently and that you realize it is hard, yet possible, to change. Pressuring the patient too hard may lead to premature termination from treatment. Use your intuition to read the patient so that you can push them or take breaks periodically as treatment progresses.

It is important to monitor the relationship with the patient. As tension develops many therapists overlook and hope the relationship improves without addressing the issue directly. Why does the therapist do this? Perhaps they feel anxiety, discomfort, and lack experience focusing on the process going on. Therapists may think it is too intrusive or aggressive to ask how the patient experiences the relationship. They may also fear that the client will say something which will undermine their confidence or sense of authority and control. In most cases, it will be helpful to ask and the patient will be given an opportunity to express themselves. For some patients, it will be too difficult or uncomfortable and they will tell you. At that point you can refocus on their treatment goals.

In conclusion it is important to highlight a few areas where boundary problems may occur. The following changes in the therapeutic relationship are red flags that problems have developed and should be addressed with a supervisor or colleague: Being lax about fees, starting sessions late or ending early, allowing extended time, gossiping about the patient with staff, drowsiness during sessions, asking patients to do favors or chores, arguing about

tangential issues with clients, unnecessary self disclosure, having appointments outside the professional setting, accepting expensive gifts, and daydreaming or fantasizing about the patient.

Cognitive Behavioral Therapy

Cognitive Behavioral therapy is widely used by clinicians to treat common presenting problems such as depression, anxiety, anger management, substance abuse and interpersonal problems. Empirical research by Albert Ellis and Aaron Beck has shown the high rates of success with this form of treatment also. These men, as well as Arnold Lazarus, are some of the pioneers in the use of Cognitive Behavioral Therapy.

The essential premise of the model is that cognitions will affect one's emotions and behavior. If a client is consistently thinking they will fail when faced with new challenges and believes they have little strength, than they will usually feel depressed and anxious. They may also avoid (behavior) new jobs, tasks, or opportunities. When the individual has rational beliefs and positive self talk, they will have more stable emotions and behavior. It is the therapist's role to uncover any misconceptions and irrational thinking patterns and to help the client adjust or counter these cognitions. Is the patient capable of doing this? The patient needs to be able to think about their thinking patterns. Many patients are able to do this, but some may resist because they prefer to ventilate their feelings and have difficulty with abstract thinking. Psychotic or Schizophrenic patients, Developmentally Delayed, Dementia patients and cognitively impaired clients will usually not benefit from Cognitive Therapy.

Some of the advantages of using this approach include its focus on: collaboration with the client, targeting specific problems, short term treatment, high rate of efficacy, empowering clients, here and now oriented, teaching the patient cognitive skills, and helping them monitor their cognitions and emotions (Turner, 1996). Patients can develop wonderful insight into their long term cognitive patterns and begin to change them in relatively short periods such as a month or two. Many of them have been aware of these patterns but did not have any way to counter these thoughts and self talk. In addition, the model is logical and fairly easy for clinicians to comprehend.

The disadvantages of this treatment include its main focus on current issues while overlooking the client's history which led up to the emotional and cognitive problems. Does the patient's childhood problems hold some clues to help solve some of their current instability? Cognitive Treatment also minimizes the need to evaluate any unconscious process that may affect the client's level of functioning. Furthermore, family dynamics are not taken into consideration as a cause of current problems.

In my own practice, I have been impressed with the efficacy of this mode of treatment. Most patients seem to comprehend it and begin to integrate the skills and ideas fairly quickly. Many need reminders to use the cognitive skills, yet can begin to experience change within one to three months. Mainly I have used it with Depressed, Anxious and Angry patients. I can recall two cases

where the patients reported that the cognitive skills were more effective in reducing their depression than their antidepressant medications. One of these patients actually discontinued his medication. A number of substance abusers have also benefitted from Cognitive treatment as well. The goal with these patients is to help them clarify triggers and thinking patterns that lead to alcohol or drug use. It is also important to assess their thoughts about relapse. If they view it as a **terrible failure** then they may slide into a long period of continued substance abuse. However, if they view it as a **small mistake** they can often recover and strengthen themselves. One way the clinician can intervene is to prepare them in case they do relapse, and to help them think about it in a rational manner. Certainly this is important since most substance abusers do relapse.

In conclusion, the Cognitive Behavioral approach is a popular treatment model which is used with a range of problems. Patients who are unable to comprehend the cognitive skills may be treated with a more behavioral model. This approach involves assessing antecedents leading to a particular behavior and what consequences follow. The model integrates the use of positive and negative reinforcements of desired or unwanted behaviors. As an example a schizophrenic adult can be given a snack after they behave well in group therapy, or a teenager can earn reward points when they control their anger during the school day. Role playing and modeling behavior can also be used. The use of daily

schedules has been effectively used for depressed or anxious patients to motivate them to exercise, seek work or participate in hobbies. Some therapists will also integrate both Cognitive techniques and Behavioral therapy and have success with this format.

FAMILY THERAPY

Prior to 1492 many explorers and map makers believed the world was flat. After Christopher Columbus made his famous journey to the Americas and reported back to Europe his findings, mostly everyone learned that the world was round. This was a paradigm shift in that people suddenly had a new perspective on the shape of the earth. In a similar way, the Family Therapy Model is a paradigm shift from the Psychodynamic or Medical Models. Therapists were beginning to view their client's problems as a result of family pathology rather than intrapsychic pathology (based on the individual's psychological problems). They also began to observe how particular interactions within the family increased or decreased the identified patient's emotional or behavioral problems. This was a major change from the focus on childhood trauma/abuse leading to later pathology. This psychodynamic perspective, which was essentially linear causation (x causes y), was in stark contrast to the Family Therapy Model.

In the 1940's, traditional psychiatry was not effective in treating schizophrenic patients or antisocial behavior. Studies were launched to evaluate family impact on mental illness. They also began to explore the use of Individual and Family therapy. Radical and profound thinkers began to emerge in the 1950's and 1960's. These included Jay Haley, Virginia Satir, Nathan Ackerman, Murray Bowen, Carl Whitaker, and Salvador Minuchin. They began to break away

from the dominant Psychoanalytic approach. In Child Guidance Clinics the focus shifted to the Mother-Child interactions. Later the whole family was invited in for therapy sessions to evaluate how they interact. In the 1960's, as the divorce rate increased, there was a stronger demand for Family treatment. At that time there was also more conduct disorder and acting out behavior among youth.

Family Therapy Theory focuses on how individuals are influenced by their families, communities and situations. Pathology is viewed as rigid and dysfunctional behavior or communication patterns. The theory strongly suggests that individuals and families have the ability to change and improve. Bowen observed and wrote about the many families he worked with who had intergenerational problems such as alcohol abuse, battering, incest and antisocial behavior. His goal in treatment was to explicate the family's behavioral and communication patterns so that they could develop insight and awareness about these trends. This would empower them to avoid the same pitfalls. Minuchin's focus was on establishing healthy boundaries within the family. He often found that the family was overly enmeshed or distancing from each other. In some families, the roles of parent and child were reversed and the children held too much authority over their passive parents. Whitaker's approach was to creatively engage the family so that they would react to him and this would lead to change. Other family clinicians will discover who the scapegoat in the family is and refocus the family members to treat them appropriately.

This form of treatment is here and now oriented, rather than focusing for many sessions on past history. The model includes an evaluation of the client in the context of their situation. It allows the patient to become empowered through self determination (making choices about change). Some techniques that are used effectively include: asking a third family member to help two others who are locked in a struggle; designing therapeutic goals and asking family members what they can do to reach those goals; offering tasks that promote risk taking for families who are rigid and dysfunctional; challenging families to prove to the therapist that they can do something; displaying genograms to point out generational patterns that are unhealthy; using therapeutic questions that hint about ways to change and possible benefits; redefining a symptom, behavior or problem in a positive way; restructuring the family so that each member understands their role and position; and focusing on measurable change rather than vague goals.

Family therapy is useful for numerous presenting problems. Empirical studies have shown that this form of treatment is useful with interpersonal conflict, parenting problems, school related problems, marital stress, sexual problems, mourning families, and intergenerational tension (Gurman and Kiniskern, 1981). Many families come to therapy focusing on a child as the identified patient. Often the child has behavioral problems or difficulty in school. They may also present with Anorexia, Asthma, Diabetes, Enuresis, Emotional problems or a Sleep Disorder. The therapist will

keep the treatment present-oriented and focus on the family's potential to change. The treatment is also cost effective in that it is usually effective within 3 to 6 months. Family therapy has been demystified through the use of video tape which is widely used for training in the field. One way mirrors are also integrated into training so new clinicians can view the process as it happens. The Ackerman Institute for Family Therapy in N.Y.C. and The Philadelphia Child Guidance Clinic are well known for their state of the art training programs.

Critics claim that Family therapy is overly focused on thinking and understanding, instead of feelings and emotions. This suggests that the clients may not feel they had a chance to ventilate. Further, the approach mainly evaluates the family interaction and overlooks the intrapsychic dimension. The developmental history is also given little attention. Critics also point out that resistance seems to be overlooked as the treatment proceeds. Lastly, will the Family therapist use this modality when it is not called for? Perhaps an example would be a case where the patient has a stable family, but long term negative thinking patterns that lead to depression. In this case, Individual Cognitive Behavioral Therapy seems to be indicated as the first choice of treatment.

Future research needs to be done to examine whether a diagnosis can be made for different types of families. These could include the distanced family, the workaholic family, the enmeshed family, the chaotic family, etc. Additional studies to pinpoint which

techniques work best with which presenting problems are needed. This could also include a focus on the clinical process and how it leads to successful outcomes. Further study on extended families and eldercare are emerging issues as the U.S. population ages. Substance abuse and its impact on family dynamics is also a growing concern. Lastly, researchers can focus on what characteristics make the family therapist effective. Are there particular personality traits that make this form of treatment work? Perhaps the engaging styles of Salvador Minuchin and Monica McGoldrick are important ingredients that lead to treatment success.

The Psychoanalytic Approach

Psychotherapy began as an exploration of underlying subconscious motivations for human behavior, communication and emotions. Sigmund Freud is well known as an original thinker who effectively treated many patients by allowing them to openly express their feelings and thoughts and helped them develop insight into their psychological problems. His work at the time was considered somewhat radical in that it was a departure from standard medical treatment.

Freud's case descriptions and theoretical writings explicate numerous psychological concepts which are critical components of the psychotherapy process. These concepts include: the defense mechanisms; transference and countertransferece; patient resistance; ego, id and superego; developmental stages, and the use of clinical interpretation. Additional psychoanalytic theorists and clinicians added to his body of work. These included his daughter Anna Freud, Alfred Adler, Otto Rank, Heinz Kohut and many others.

Defense mechanisms are often used by patients as a way to cope with anxiety which develops when there is a conflict between the Id (aggressive and sexual drives) and the Superego (moral core). The defense helps the individual handle unacceptable impulses or fears that develop. In most cases, the defense is not chosen by the client but arises from the unconscious process. The client will not plan to use denial, for example, when they are trying to face a

difficult situation. More likely, their defenses will distort reality. At times, the defense can be adaptive and help them cope with a severe experience. A patient who is informed that he has cancer will often exhibit denial about the diagnosis. This is functional because it helps him absorb the information and possible life changes. However, if the denial prevents him from accepting the medical problem, then he may avoid medical treatment. This is obviously dysfunctional. Therapists will often confront their patient's defenses, and they in turn, usually resist this approach. Direct confrontation, without a strong therapeutic alliance, can lead the patient to exhibit angry outbursts, withdrawal or premature termination. It is critical that the clinician is sensitive and careful when they explore and reveal the patients habitual defenses. Lastly, defenses are conditioned responses that often develop in childhood. They may also be learned responses in that the child may copy some of the defensive patterns of a parental figure.

Patients are using the defense called **repression** when they keep unwanted thoughts or memories out of their awareness. Usually the memory is of a traumatic event such as a murder, severe accident, etc. **Regression** is revealed when the client turns back to a lower level of functioning or behaviors as a way to cope with present anxiety. Adult patients who feel overwhelmed may exhibit regression by rocking back and forth, playing with toys, hugging a teddy bear or biting their hand. Children may also regress to earlier developmental stages. As an example a ten year old child may

regress by sucking their thumb again or taking daytime naps. **Sublimation** is used to convert sexual or aggressive impulses into an acceptable activity. Some highly sexualized males will choose jobs where they can focus on women such as clothing design or hairdressing. Others may channel their aggressive energy into sports or law enforcement. **Rationalization** is commonly used to justify one's ideas or behavior while blocking out the underlying motive. Clients may rationalize their antisocial behavior by describing how everyone they know takes things from work. **Displacement** is a defense that involves shifting one's feelings about someone onto another person. A classic scenario is the worker who feels angry at his supervisor, but too anxious to express himself directly. He then goes home and yells at his wife. An insightful spouse may become aware of this process and point it out to him. Clients who convert intolerable or strong impulses into physical problems are displaying **somatization**. Usually they become intensely focused on their somatic problems and this may prevent them from exploring the more difficult psychological issues.

A central thesis of the psychoanalytic model is the connection between childhood trauma or abuse and future psychopathology. Freud often uncovered his patient's prior emotional, sexual or physical abuse and found that it was highly correlated to the development of personality disorders, emotional disorders, dissociation, and behavioral problems. His work, and the other early psychoanalysts, opened the door to evaluate and understand the

causal links between abuse and long term psychiatric problems. Currently, clinical research clearly shows that a significant number of children and adults suffer abuse and need treatment to cope with their emotions and memories.

Critics point out that psychoanalytic treatment takes too long and is expensive. There is also limited empirical research which shows the approach is effective. Some of the limitations also include vague treatment goals, unfocused sessions and difficulty evaluating if clinician's interpretations are accurate or helpful to patients. Clinical training is quite extensive and has a mysterious quality compared to family therapy training which is more transparent with one way mirrors and video taping capacities.

Solution-Focused Therapy

Traditional therapy focused on the past to explore childhood history that may reveal root causes of present problems. Family therapy, behavioral therapy, and ego psychology focus more on the present. The goal was to find out what maintains the current problem. Solution-focused therapy focuses on the future. The key question within this approach is how can problems be solved? Treatment explores what works and what are the client's strengths or abilities that can be used to change the problem or situation. Many of the current solution focused therapists and experts base their work on the original ideas of Milton Erikson. He was a psychotherapist and hypnotherapist and had great success with a wide range of clients. Erikson suggested that clients have a reservoir of wisdom and skills that are learned and forgotten. The therapist helps them uncover their strengths and begin to think, behave and interact differently (O'Hanlon, 1995).

The therapist will act like a gardener who uses everything the patient presents, including the weeds. These weeds may be resistance, various symptoms, rigid beliefs, compulsive behaviors, etc. The goal is to integrate these weeds into part of the solution. Therapeutic questions are also employed to explore future possibilities and areas of potential change. The miracle question has been effectively used with patients. The client is asked: If you were to wake up tomorrow and all your problems were gone how

would you describe your life? The patient may then describe an emotionally stable life with improved social contact. This will help the therapist design small steps that he can take as part of the solution. The exception question is also used to uncover when the client is doing well. The client is asked: When have you noticed that you don't have your problem? This helps the client discover solutions they forgot or didn't notice. The therapist may also find clues that are solution-focused. As an example, a depressed patient may remember that they felt calm and stable when they were jogging daily last year or when they visited their friend two times a week. This suggests they need to maintain an exercise routine and regular social contact. Part of this approach is to amplify when things are going well and help the client realize what works. One small change can lead to quick dramatic change. An anxious client who tries something new and feels successful will often want to try something else and build on their optimism.

This treatment perspective also assesses how the patient or family views their presenting problem. If the parents of a child who walks out of his classroom without permission view him as rebellious, they will take steps to punish him. If they view it as a learning or social problem, they may take him to the school counselor. If they see it as a medical problem (chemical imbalance leading to hyperactivity), they may seek medication from a psychiatrist. Changing the family's view of the situation may lead to more effective solutions.

In addition, action related to the problem can be targeted. If the parents usually yell at their child when they have a temper tantrum the parents can be encouraged to do something else like ignoring the behavior. This could lead to extinction of the negative behavior. The goal is to avoid unsuccessful behavioral patterns. At times, strengths and skills are revealed when the interactions are changed or shifted. Couples who pick on each other and complain can be given the task of randomly surprising each other in some positive ways. The other spouse is given the task of trying to spot the new behavior. In this way, the husband is given the task of trying new behaviors and he knows it will be recognized. The task also has a playful quality which is healthy for the tense relationship. This can lead to a solution since they have shifted from their focus on problems and complaints.

Solution-focused therapy is used as a way to empower clients to change. The therapist also takes the stance that change will happen. Questions such as: What do you think you will be doing when your panic attacks decrease? are commonly asked. This helps the patient begin to feel that change is possible. The focus is mainly on strengths rather than pathology. Clinicians stay goal oriented throughout treatment and set up goals in collaboration with the client. The treatment is usually short term and is most effective when the patient is motivated to change and willing to try new things.

Critics report that many clients are highly resistant and incapable of trying new behaviors or ways to communicate. Further, the model

overlooks the patient's developmental history, unconscious processes, and long term defenses. The model does evaluate cognitions, behaviors and emotions which play a role in maintaining the presenting problem. Empirical studies have reported excellent results using this approach for family problems, behavioral problems and some emotional disorders (O'Hanlon, 1995). Many therapists enjoy using solution focused treatment because it is creative and positively oriented.

ECLECTIC PRACTICE

Many clinicians employ a variety of techniques and theories as they practice psychotherapy with their clients. Some will begin treatment using a specific theory or approach and will switch to another treatment modality if no improvement develops. Perhaps they begin with solution-focused treatment and have little success. They may then switch to cognitive-behavioral therapy and find it is more effective. This approach is humane in that the clinician moves on from an unsuccessful therapy to a new approach. Why continue to treat without any significant effect? Of course the therapist has to be well trained and comfortable with several types of treatment approaches in order to do this.

The eclectic model also integrates many perspectives into one umbrella approach. One can view the client in terms of their interpersonal problems, intrapsychic struggles and cognitive distortions. This multidimensional perspective may be more accurate in clarifying the patients overall problems. Many therapists who use the eclectic model report that it gives them flexibility and creative freedom. Some clinicians who only treat clients with one therapeutic approach may feel bored or worn down as they repeat the same questions and line of thought. Of course, using one mode of treatment may be advantageous in that the therapist can develop seasoned clinical skills.

The eclectic perspective, which is not a theory in itself, suggests that therapists select from a variety of effective treatment models how they will treat different clients. This approach promotes creativity, careful assessment of the individual's needs and innovation. Rosen (cited in Dorfman, 1988) posits that this metaparadigm encourages clinicians to choose theories which are cost effective, produce changes in the client's functioning, are falsifiable, and are comprehensible.

The eclectic approach relies on the empirical evidence which has been uncovered by the various models such as psychodynamic, cognitive-behavioral, and family therapy theory. Researchers in the field of eclecticism have recognized important common elements within the well founded theories. These include the importance of the client-therapist relationship, assessment of the client's interpersonal and intrapsychic problems, and the focus on the client's potential for growth and change.

It is clear that the therapeutic modalities must be carefully chosen so they match the needs of the patient. Therapists who strive to maintain an eclectic approach need to be well trained and well read in the various theories and clinical techniques. Without proper training they may incorrectly employ the model or interventions and have poor results.

The advantages of using an eclectic model are important to clarify. Using a variety of treatment models gives the therapist an opportunity to focus on both intrapsychic and interpersonal issues.

This gives a more rounded approach to treatment and prevents missing critical dynamics that affect the client's level of functioning. The eclectic approach is also exciting for the clinician because they have numerous models and techniques to choose from. This helps prevent burnout for them.

MEDICATION AND PSYCHOTHERAPY

The use of medication in conjunction with psychotherapy has been a controversial issue. Perhaps the patient will avoid the therapeutic challenge of working on his or her problems if they overly rely on their medication to solve their difficulties. Many patients discontinue therapy and put all of their hope into the medications. However, there is strong evidence that the combined use of medication and psychotherapy is the most effective treatment for a wide range of clinical disorders. Medications alone can reduce depression, anxiety, anger and psychotic symptoms in approximately 70% to 80% of clients who take them. These results are excellent and usually the patients have minimal side effects from the psychiatric medications. If they do, it is usually mild, such as headaches, stomachaches, dry mouth or reduced libido.

Patients who present with severe emotional disorders, such as depression or anxiety, will usually improve within two to four months when they are prescribed the proper medications, the therapist then has an easier time working with the patient on enhancing their level of functioning and relational issues. Certainly the medications don't solve all of their problems but they often give the patient more energy and motivation to begin taking risks and being more active. Psychotherapy adds the human touch; the clients usually need psychological and emotional encouragement as they begin to make changes in their life.

Many patients report that their medications are not effective. This needs to be carefully explored. When questioned, the patients often report that they discontinued taking the pills before they began to be effective. Many antidepressant medications, such as Prozac and Zoloft, take three to six weeks to begin working. Other patients reveal that they don't actually take their pills daily as prescribed and they will therefore be less potent. Some may be abusing alcohol, cannabis or other drugs while they take their psychiatric medications and this will also reduce the benefits of the pills. It is also common for patients to have many questions about their medications. Many of them also have fear and embarrassment about asking their doctor for advice. They may fear the doctor because they are in an authority position or because they don't want to take the doctor's time. Psychotherapists need to explore these feelings and help them address these issues and begin communicating more openly with their doctors.

Therapists need to evaluate their view of psychiatric medications. The following are key questions to explore and think about:
Do you dismiss medications as unhelpful? Have you reviewed the empirical literature in support of medications? Do you view the long term use of medications as disabling (maintaining the help seeker in the patient role)? Are you concerned about long term side effects? What assumptions do you make about medications and is there any evidence to support your opinion?

CLINICAL CASES

In all of the following cases, client names have been changed.

The Anxious Painter

A 30 year male, named Bill, presented with anxiety after being attacked by another male about four months prior to seeking help. He was planning to press charges against him and felt vulnerable. His family and girlfriend were supportive. Bill had never attended any treatment before. In terms of employment, he was a house painter for the past ten years. In general he described himself as easy going and content with his work and social activities prior to the trauma. In the first few sessions it was clear that he had catastrophic thoughts about being attacked or mugged again. He felt fearful of men and avoided leaving his home or talking with men. His anxiety was moderate to severe and he felt frustrated. Bill's relationship with his girlfriend was also strained and his sleep was inconsistent.

The main focus of therapy was on helping him clarify his cognitions and how they led to anxiety, fear and avoidance behavior. Bill was cooperative with treatment and began taking anti-anxiety medications also. Cognitive therapy was mildly helpful and he began to do some work and travel alone. He was learning to counter his fearful thoughts and expectations that something would happen to him. Periodically he felt anxious when speaking to men and would abruptly leave a painting job if he felt vulnerable. As a way to improve his functional level I suggested that he hire a

male teenager who he could trust to assist him with his work and to help him feel less isolated and vulnerable. This proved to be helpful and he discontinued leaving jobs due to fear. He also began to carry pepper spray so that he could defend himself if anyone tried to take advantage of him. Treatment was effective for Bill because he felt empowered and capable of protecting himself, if necessary.

Female with HIV

Linda was a 39 year old single mother who contracted HIV from her long term boyfriend. He died several years ago. She recently found out about her diagnosis and was shocked and depressed. Linda was also angry at herself and her situation. She had always been highly ambitious and goal oriented and this medical disorder was viewed as a major block to her goals. In the first few sessions she ventilated angrily. She was also raising a 12 year old daughter and felt it was unfair for her daughter to have a sick mother. One of the most difficult problems was that she felt very isolated and distanced from others. Part of the problem was that she was pulling away from everyone else. She thought that because of her HIV no one would want to be with her or to have a romantic relationship with her. Her cognitions were firm. My approach was to softly question her assumptions about others. I also gave examples of others who came to our clinic and were able to develop a social life even though they had HIV. She was surprised to hear about others who were

accepted in social circles and even capable of developing a love life. Her sense of self and cognitions began to change over the next few months of therapy. Her emotional pain decreased and her self esteem improved. Soon after she met a man working at an office she attended and began dating. She was very pleased that he still accepted her even after she revealed that she was HIV positive. They were engaged within the year.

This case was an excellent example of how a change in cognitions can affect the patient's emotions and behavior.

<u>The Histrionic Female</u>

Jackie was a 60 year old divorced female who had numerous complaints. She was sexually abused by her father as a child and had flashbacks and depression for many years. She also had ongoing interpersonal problems with her two adult children and men she dated. Jackie was very needy and narcissistic. She used externalization as a defense. In essence, she blamed others for most of her problems. This way she could avoid the difficulty of having to change herself. Most clients who attend treatment exhibit some of this pattern.

Jackie was given many sessions to ventilate her feelings and reactions to the people in her life. Of course she would be unable to change without looking at herself. Once the therapeutic alliance was established after five sessions, I began to slowly shift the

therapeutic focus. Periodically I would ask, "What do you think you could be doing differently when interacting with the people in your life to improve the relationships.?" As expected she would dodge this question. My goal was to get her to start thinking about her own impact on others. I asked this question about four or five times over a number of sessions. Finally she came to a later session and began by stating that she had been thinking about my question and realized that she may have a negative impact on others when she starts screaming and demanding things. This was a major breakthrough for her and led to further exploration of her behavior and interactions. In essence, she was developing a stronger observing ego with the help of the therapist. The main function of the observing ego is to objectively evaluate oneself. Treatment continued with a focus on evaluating new ways to communicate with others and observing their reactions to her.

<u>The Antisocial Male</u>

John, a 29 year old single male, was mandated to attend treatment because he had been selling drugs. The therapy goal was to review his past behavior and discontinue all antisocial behavior. He was a good candidate for therapy because he felt remorse about his behavior. In group therapy he revealed that he had been gainfully employed but tried to make extra money selling drugs. The temptation to make quick money had been too strong.

John also revealed that his mother attended court when he was found guilty and sentenced to one year in jail. This was one of the most humiliating experiences for him. He could not even look at her as he was taken out of the court room. John was instructed to describe this experience in detail and remember it. In this way if he ever had the urge to sell drugs or do any other antisocial activities he would recall the consequences. John successfully reentered the work force over the next few months.

The Depressed Male

Ethan was a 30 year old College student who had felt depressed most of his life. He had vague recollections of being emotionally abused by his older brothers. Ethan began with weekly psychotherapy and Prozac daily from his psychiatrist. His mood improved slightly over the next few months. He continued with College classes but had trouble with low energy and wavering concentration. Certainly he was intelligent and had done very well in many of his classes. After exploring his past history of abuse Ethan was introduced to the basic concepts of cognitive behavioral therapy and began to evaluate his daily cognitions. He was a quick study and soon spotted numerous negative cognitive patterns. He was criticizing himself throughout the day and feeling hopeless at times. He was given an assignment to record these thoughts and see what triggers might lead to them. He soon found that when he felt lonely

or unsuccessful at school, his self criticism would intensify. Together we began to work on ways to counter these negative thinking patterns. He made a long list of his positive traits and abilities and reviewed it to enhance his self esteem. Soon he was able to identify negative cognitions and to counter them with more hopeful and rational thoughts. His mood improved quickly and his grades stabilized at College.

Ethan continued on antidepressant medication for about two years. He contacted me after moving to another state and reported that he discontinued the Prozac and was feeling emotionally stable. He was using the cognitive skills we worked on and found that they were the key to his improvement. This was the first case where a patient reported that the therapy skills were more helpful than the medication.

Couples Therapy

Bill, age 25, and Lisa, age 37, came to therapy due to marital problems. They were raising Bill's brother's four year old son. Bill left his wife twice during their first year of marriage to live with an old girlfriend. Each time he visited this woman he stayed with her for one month. Lisa felt worried and frustrated. She was unsure if she could trust him.

Lisa had been previously married for three years. She was divorced many years ago and had no children from that

relationship. She had been beaten by her first husband. She was working in sales and doing fairly well. Bill never finished High School and had a poor work history. He had gone from job to job and often quit when frustrated. Sometimes he was fired for poor work performance. His obvious strength was his sense of humor. He had low self esteem and a limited observing ego. Lisa appeared to be intelligent and empathic.

Bill grew up in a family were his father, an alcoholic, beat his mother severely. Bill retreated from the chaos at home by hiding in his room and listening to Elvis Presley music for hours. As a child he sometimes thought he was loosing his identity and becoming Elvis. He also experienced this as an adult. Bill had long sideburns and a deep voice which are obvious characteristics of Elvis. Certainly he used music as an escape. He appeared to have dissociative disorder traits.

Bill was distancing (isolating himself and listening to music) from his wife to avoid conflict. Bill reported that when he tried to communicate openly with his family as a child, he was often betrayed. This made him feel mistrustful and affected his ability to communicate with his wife. We learned about his sensitivity when he discussed how he felt betrayed when Lisa told her family about some of their personal problems. He felt angry and embarrassed about it. My goal was to use therapeutic questions to promote understanding between them. Questions focusing on past ways of functioning

within their family of origin helps the spouse comprehend why their partner acts and thinks the way they do.

Lisa felt insecure about Bill and his ability to stay faithful. I asked her, "What does he have to do to make up for what he has done?" This can be helpful because it suggests that she can forgive him and encourages her to ask for what she needs. Lisa clarified that she needs to feel safe, loved and wanted in the marriage.

As therapy continued, a variety of questions were used to hint to them what they could do to improve their relationship. As an example I asked, "Do you feel that the trust in your relationship is tarnished when Bill looks for a retreat outside your marriage with his old girlfriend?" Lisa responded by describing the pain she suffered when he would do that. Bill began to acknowledge the impact of his behavior on her. They were also asked "what makes a good marriage?" In this way they were encouraged to discuss their needs, hopes, and expectations of each other. In order to help them monitor their behavior they were also asked, "What impact do you think your behavior will have on your child as he grows up?" When tension increased they were asked "What originally attracted you to your spouse?" This was used at the end of a session so they would leave feeling positively about each other.

Another disturbing issue came up involving Bill's sister. She would pressure him for financial help periodically. Lisa wanted him to set limits with her since they were financially strained. Bill began to take an objective view of his role as fix-it man in his family of origin. He

began to prioritize when he would help his wife and when to help his family. He was encouraged to speak with his sister about his own limitations. Lisa was supportive as he moved in this direction. As familial boundaries were developing the couple felt closer. Bill started to give himself permission to help his immediate family rather than be dragged into his sister's problems. Later they revealed that she was a gambler and used guilt inducing maneuvers to get his help. Another problem was Bill's low frustration tolerance at work. Lisa was encouraged to help him ventilate his feelings about work stress and offer solutions. This helped remind them that they are a valuable resource to each other.

Within two months, this couple made significant changes in their relationship with each other and their family. They were challenged by the therapist to maintain these changes and given the opportunity to return if they felt the need. The key to treatment was maintaining a neutral stance with the couple and using questions to explore possibilities and ways to change.

Stuck feeling Guilty

Liza was a fifty year old single female who presented with moderate depression. She was living alone and mainly spending her time caring for her elderly father who was in a nursing home. He had severe dementia and she visited him daily. She began Cognitive Behavioral therapy with me and was prescribed Paxil by her

psychiatrist. Her two main problems were her chronic self ridicule/guilt over how she mistreated her father and her inability to reenter the workforce. She had worked for many years doing office work and career counseling. She also had low self esteem and had avoided dating anyone for the last five years. It soon became clear that she was trying to correct her past wrongs by overcompensating. She felt guilty for verbally abusing her father on a few occasions when he initially developed dementia. She was actually angrier at the medical problem than at him. Further, she resisted change and had persistent critical cognitions about herself.

Liza was introduced to cognitive behavioral concepts and assignments and was soon monitoring her cognitions. She began to comprehend how often her negative cognitions led to guilt, depression, and anger. She was helped to view her past verbal abuse of her father as a limited period where she was not behaving well. However, I pointed out how she had been an exceptionally dedicated daughter for the majority of the time that she cared for him. After one and a half years of treatment her depression was reduced from moderate to mild. At that point her father died and she began to mourn for the next three months. Liza came in for a session and said she felt that her fever had broken, meaning her depression and self ridicule were ending. She was feeling motivated to seek a job and take better care of herself (It is interesting to note that she was wearing makeup and jewelry that day which was uncommon for her).

Several critical interventions helped Liza begin the process of change. She was taught to monitor and counter her negative thinking patterns. She was challenged to change herself and not to expect anyone to do it for her. And she was given time limitations in treatment so that she would feel some pressure to start making changes. In addition, her assumption that she needed to uncover some crucial underlying issues was also challenged because it was viewed as a form of resistance and avoidance of the hard work of changing.

The Depressed Dissociating Client

Sue, age 32, is a shy Hispanic female who suffers from depression, anxiety, and psychotic symptoms. She describes herself as being confused. She has limited pleasure. The client appears to be holding down her emotions to prevent a flood of tears. The sounds and voices that she hears and the shadows that she sees make her feel crazy. Sue has experienced these ego dystonic hallucinations for the past two years. In terms of her ego strengths she is empathic and cares greatly for her daughters. Her father died five months before she came for treatment. Even though he had been an alcoholic and emotionally abusive to her she still suffered a great loss when he died. Sue presently lives with a boyfriend, George, who she has known for the past two years. They have not had any children together. However, this client has three daughters ages 16, 13, and

12, who she cares for at her home. Each child had a different father and Sue has never married. She had an eighth grade education and is currently collecting welfare benefits.

The client's original diagnosis was Major Depression, severe, with Psychotic Features and Borderline Personality traits. In terms of medication, the psychiatrist prescribed Pamelor, Xanax, and Loxitane. These medications are useful to decrease depression, anxiety and psychotic symptoms.

Feeling distrustful and fragile, Sue began psychotherapy sessions. She needed encouragement to express her thoughts and feelings. The most stressful issue she faced involved her mother and sister. According to Sue's reports they treated her cruelly and tried to sabotage her life. The client distanced herself from them but was often pulled back into the family system when crises erupted. Sue felt fortunate that her boyfriend was supportive during these emotionally draining periods.

Agoraphobia is also a problem for her. She feels paranoid and fearful of leaving her home alone. Her psychotic symptoms intensified and she began to have suicidal thoughts. A psychiatric consultation was quickly arranged and Sue was admitted to the psychiatric unit of the hospital for close monitoring.

After two weeks in the inpatient unit she was released. Therapy began to focus on trust between the therapist and client. Educative work about the purpose of therapy was also initiated. As treatment progressed she began to develop some trust with the clinician. Sue

was helped to evaluate her life in the context of person-in-environment. Sue felt lonely and cut off from her mother. She missed her father who had been the peacekeeper in the family. In the past he intervened and protected her from the mother's and sister's insults. Sue was presently disliked by her family because she would not take in her alcoholic brothers when her mother would throw them out. She exhibited strength setting limits with them, but suffered emotionally in the process. The therapist supported her stance with her family as she sorely needed someone to align with her. This, in turn, enhanced the therapeutic alliance.

In the following session Sue described periodic episodes where she felt outside her body. She also described various personality changes. Sue would dress differently at times or use makeup in a strange manner. Fearful and confused, she reported that she experienced these changes over the past fifteen years but was afraid to speak about them. The client denied being physically or sexually abused. It appeared that she was possibly repressing some memories or not feeling comfortable enough to explore her past. Perhaps she was dissociating as a defense. Clients may deny or minimize their dissociating experiences as a form of defense.

Sue appeared to have Post Traumatic Stress Disorder and Dissociative traits. She reported that she did not always recognize herself when looking in the mirror, another dissociative symptom. She also began to tell more about her childhood problems. As a seven year old girl her brother, age 17, repeatedly abused her sexually.

When she told her parents about it, they hit her or sent her to bed. In therapy she revealed that she often had out of body experiences when the abuse took place. Sue harbored confusion, anger, and disappointment about her family. In addition, she would loose track of time for up to one hour. Sue also found new clothing in her closet on six occasions, which she could not recall buying or receiving as gifts. The therapist discussed the possibility that she has another personality that may purchase these clothes.

It is important to note that the therapist needs to be cognizant of the type of questions he/she asks clients as they begin to reveal their history of abuse or imagined abuse. Leading questions and statements such as, "I imagine that you must have been severely abused as a child since you appear so fragile now" can highly influence clients. Some clinicians may inappropriately interpret dreams which may encourage clients to report false memories.

In a later session, Sue reported that she was kidnapped for three days by a male neighbor when she was four years old. She was physically and sexually abused by him. Once released, her family did not press charges, but rather sent her to family in Puerto Rico. Since she felt abandoned by her parents after this event, and the abuse by her brother, her shame, guilt, loneliness, and confusion were compounded. This contributed to a poor self image and difficulty forming trusting relationships, especially with men. She felt distraught and extremely vulnerable. Sue still harbored resentment toward this neighbor and her parents who did protect her from this

abuse. Keeping this all secret for so long had been emotionally taxing.

Between sessions she heard muted voices which sounded as if they were in her head. This is typical of patients who dissociate. On the other hand, psychotic patients usually hear voices coming from outside themselves. Sue generally stayed home and was fearful of going out.

An additional trauma involved her brother. At age 18 she was sitting with him on their front porch when he was suddenly shot and killed. Sue was in shock for several days and cannot recall much of this event. Certainly she suffered through severe traumatic events as a child and adult. When she would cry in sessions her deep emotional pain was apparent. However, Sue's developing ability to express herself was a sign of improvement. For most of her life she was blaming herself for much of the abuse that she had experience-ed. Treatment strategy focused on helping her take an objective view of the past and to decrease her self blaming. Through an evaluation of her positive traits and abilities Sue's self esteem began to improve. Her emotional pain began to decrease as she told her life story. As she developed an improved sense of self, she began to speak about making positive changes in her life. Soon Sue was concerned about her boyfriend who was reacting to her struggle for change. He was thrown off balance as she tried to change her needy role in their relationship. Unfortunately he was unwilling to come in for couples therapy.

Sue began to focus more on her agoraphobia. She was given an assignment to go out for short walks by herself. The therapist explained that she could go home if her anxiety level increased. Within weeks she was encouraged to take walks for one block, then two blocks, etc. Sue slowly developed self confidence in this area and took longer walks alone. This behavioral / task oriented approach was effective because the client felt successful doing small tasks which then gave her courage and motivation to try more advanced tasks.

During the last two sessions, termination issues were highlighted. She had decreased her self blaming thoughts and her confidence was higher. Also, she was not reporting any episodes of dissociation or hallucinations. Even though a trusting relationship had been established with this therapist, she was having difficulty expressing any emotional feelings about the relationship. Her traumatic past had stifled her emotions and her ability to develop close inter-personal relationships.

The main ingredients in therapy were compassion, empathy, and validation of Sue's feelings. She exhibited fragility, yet through a process of ego strengthening her sense of self improved. The clinician continually encouraged her to focus on her positive traits and abilities. This helped her develop the capability to be self nurturing and begin the process of restructuring her self image. Through educative work she learned about her disorder which, in turn, decreased her fears and confusion.

The Narcissistic Male

Jose was a 42 year old self focused male, who had intense marital problems. When meeting with him for the first time the therapist had in mind the principle that the therapeutic session itself is a reflection of the client's life and way of functioning. He focused on himself for nearly the entire session. At the end of the meeting he quickly mentioned that he was married and had a four year old son. Sensed immediately was his narcissism and feelings of isolation. As a young child he was physically abused by his parents and suffered the trauma of his mother's death from heart failure when he was ten years old. Overburdened with having to care for his younger brother and depressed for much of his childhood, Jose harbored feelings of anger, resentment, and self pity, gaining strength by focusing on his intelligence.

This client appeared to have compensated for his past emotional deprivation by becoming narcissistic. In an impressive way he had made personality adjustments and maintained a high level of functioning socially and as a wage earner. Due to his narcissistic traits he would need to be treated respectfully and carefully in sessions. Jose described his life with his wife as rocky and intense. She would rarely do what he wanted. He explained that he would have to beg just to get her to make side dishes with dinner. The therapist appealed to his narcissism and encouraged him to empathize with her, since he sounded like the mature half of the

couple. Later, he clarified that he had strong emotional reactions or no feelings at all when dealing with his family. We also discussed his goal of developing an internal thermostat for his feelings and reactions. Jose needed to control his emotional outbursts so that his feelings would be more acceptable and understandable to those around him.

The approach to treatment was to be accepting and empathic. It was hoped that modeling would help the client develop greater empathy. In addition, through transference, it was imagined that Jose would see his therapist as a parental figure. Jose described how much he wanted to feel accepted when he stated, "I just want someone to say I am o.k." Therapy focused on listening to Jose, confirming his feelings, and avoiding any form of confrontation.

At times, Jose felt suicidal and hopeless. He said that he "converts his emotional pain into anger." He could cope with the anger but not the pain. During this period he obviously needed much support and used sessions to ventilate freely. Fortunately, the client felt dedicated to being a responsible father and husband and this prevented him from following through with suicide. In addition, Jose took pride in the fact that he did not physically abuse his family in any way. Occasionally he was given genuine compliments which he had trouble accepting. He explained that his parents gave him mixed messages (compliments and ridicule) and that he often cannot believe people when they compliment him, even if he knows it is true.

This theme of mistrust and protecting himself from others became more evident as therapy entered the fourth month. Jose seemed to be protecting himself from others and setting up barriers. He was apparently using his logic skills to defend himself from those around him. He impressed as always having to be right and would debate over trivial matters. The therapist realized that insight oriented interventions were construed as offensive to Jose.

He continued to express how much love and support he missed as a child. Many times he said that he needed more love from his wife. Therapy was conceptualized as a way to give the client the support he needed in order to be less demanding on his wife.

As the fifth month of treatment was reached, he arrived in the office and said, "I have a friend at work who really seems to care about me and I told him thanks." Perhaps his protective wall was breaking down enough for him to perceive this closeness. Later in that session his narcissistic quality emerged and he said, "I'm advancing a lot in therapy, more than my wife. She needs improvement." Even though he was ridiculing his wife, it was good to hear he felt successful in treatment. A few weeks later he described how he told his wife and coworkers on two occasions, "thanks for putting up with me." He was gaining clarity about his impact on others.

During the sixth month of treatment, Jose regressed in several ways. When he asked his wife to do things he went into angry rages and threatened to leave her. Jose interpreted his wife's requests as

demands and this in turn brought up bitter memories of his parents demanding his obedience with household chores. Jose also discussed his fear of his wife and the power he felt she had over him at times. He explained that she says things that make him feel unloved and this, sometimes, causes him to feel depressed. Jose imagined it would be better to get divorced and escape from his powerless role. The therapist tried to calm him and affirm his feelings. Jose did not follow through with the separation or divorce but did use three sessions to ventilate emotionally.

It is important to point out that narcissistic clients can function well when they feel wanted and admired. However, if their grandiosity is challenged they can become angry, filled with rage, and possibly aggressive. In some cases, they will also become depressed.

In his eighth month of therapy Jose spoke about his philosophy of childrearing. His main focus was to bring up his son properly, with care and concern. Jose also did not want to overburden him with household duties as he had been when he was a child. The client exhibited pride and empathy when speaking about his son. He also brought up his feelings of sympathy toward neglected city children. Perhaps, Jose imagined, one day he could teach or coach these kids. A week later, he shared the extent of his caring thoughts for others. He had attended group therapy for men several times and described an incident with a young graduate of a master's level music program. This group member was depressed because his

father told him now that he graduated he could get him a job in a bank. Jose told this man, "Well, I'm proud of you for finishing. You go out and get the best job you can in the music field." The client explained that he wanted to give him the support he wished his own father had given him. Encouraged by this experience Jose continued in this direction.

A few weeks later, Jose spoke about a group member, Ed, who needed open heart surgery. No one in the group had spoken about the pending operation or their thoughts about it. Jose asked the members, "How does everyone feel about it?" After a short discussion Ed asked, "Can I return to the group even if I am hospitalized for an extended period of time?" Jose responded, "To me you will always be part of the group." In that same session Jose spoke about his anger towards his father and how he was physically abused. He said, "how can I totally blame my father, he was abused as a child also." He was beginning to see things from different perspectives.

After fifteen months of therapy, this client began to reveal a warm and caring personality. Jose had rarely been able to discuss his feelings about his therapist in the sessions, but in the final meeting he said, "I will miss these sessions." He also stated that he had clearly learned what not to do to his son from his own childhood.

This case was productive because of the clinical focus on the client's feelings and reactions to others. The therapist gently worked with the client to help him explore his past as well as his current

struggles. As the client received needed support in therapy he was able to change how he interacts with those around him.

The Enuretic Child

Bob and Nancy were a middle class family who came to the first session with their children. Their son, Jimmy, was eight years old and their daughter, Susan was four. The parents, both in their thirties, complained about Jimmy's daytime enuresis problem. They described him as temperamental, poorly organized, and clumsy. Jimmy stated that he felt alone and unable to please his parents. Bob had a good work history as an engineer. This was the only marriage for Bob and Nancy. She presented as a well organized woman who was busy as a homemaker and part time secretary.

After gathering information about this family, the clinician began to formulate therapeutic strategies and interventions. It is important to assess what a family has previously tried to do to handle their problems. Have they been successful at all? What changes would they like to see? What developments do the children hope for in the family? Therapists can gather much information about the way family systems work through this type of questioning. Also are family members giving each other mixed messages? If so, therapists need to formulate interventions to clarify the impact of these communications. Furthermore, one must evaluate the level of

respect and decide if educative work about respecting each other is indicated.

As treatment progresses, family problems that focus on children often lead to reveal marital conflict. An essential ingredient in treatment is to follow the pace of the family and avoid rushing them into marital therapy. It is common that as layers of conflict peel away and the couple realize that they need treatment they will exhibit resistance to working on their relationship. Sometimes such couples will return in the future for help when they feel psychologically ready.

In this enuretic case, physical problems were ruled out by a recent medical exam. With this in mind, the clinician must search for reasons behind the presenting problem. In many cases enuresis develops because of something that creates anxiety or because of family tension. An environmental stressor may also affect the child's bladder control.

The Strategic family therapy model was used to treat this case. The focus was to create experiences in the sessions that would have a strong impact on the family and their view of each other. The sessions needed to be enjoyable because the father and son were not enthusiastic about attending. It was clear that Bob and Jimmy had similar personality characteristics. The therapist wondered if, perhaps, the father disliked seeing certain traits of his own in his son.

The first intervention was to encourage Bob, when he felt ready, to explain to his son that when he says, " I might give you to another

family if you behave so badly," he really means that he is frustrated. Bob was helped to see that he was undermining his own efforts to solve the wetting problems by increasing anxiety and fear in his son. Bob surprised the therapist by readily agreeing to speak with Jimmy about these threats to give him away. He told him that he will always love him and that he will stop the threats of giving him away. The clinician was impressed with the intensity of the discussion and pleased to see them hug each other.

During therapy, it became clear that the family members were able to reevaluate their view of the initial problem. Hopefully this would decrease much of the tension and fear that Jimmy had been feeling. Many families tend to focus on one big presenting problem during the beginning of therapy. Later, as they become more open and honest, other interconnected problems emerge.

In order to help the father become more involved with his children, a quarter game was played during the next meeting. Bob was told to hide two quarters somewhere in his shoes or clothes secretly. The kids were then given the chance to find the quarters, and as hoped, they tickled their father in the process. This reminded the family that they can be playful and enjoy each others company. Other activities that they can play for fun were also discussed.

In further sessions, Nancy was encouraged to defend her husband if the children are disrespectful to him and Bob was to do the same for her. Bob stayed home for five days during winter vacation and related well with his wife and children, particularly

when they went out on several outings. Throughout treatment the therapist rarely asked about the enuresis problem. The parents did relate that during the vacation week Jimmy had no accidents. These parents turned to the therapist as if he had all the power to affect change. It was explained that parents have more power and influence than anyone outside the family, especially when they are a united front.

As meetings continued it became apparent that Bob harbored feelings of depression and was lethargic at times. Nancy described him as inconsistent and always late. She brought up a new goal in therapy. She hoped he would try to overcome his depression and improve his level of responsibility in the family. Bob agreed and said he wanted to work on these issues, and added that their marriage needed help.

Soon they began to come to sessions without their children and focused on their own needs. Nancy wanted him to be more considerate of her feelings. She wanted more attention and felt Bob was distancing himself. He appeared to create space between them. He had some worries that he would loose her and the family unless he tried harder to be more responsible to his family. Predictions about slipping back to his old ways were made and Bob took up the challenge by saying that he would push himself continuously. After four months we had a termination session to discuss the positive impact of their newly developed marital

harmony on their children and Jimmy's improved sense of security and comfort in the family.

RECURRENT MAJOR DEPRESSION:

Clinical social workers commonly treat clients who exhibit chronic emotional problems such as depression or anxiety. These clients can be draining, demanding and needy. Therapists often struggle to help these individuals overcome their affective disorders and to improve their level of functioning. It is important that therapeutic strategies are clear, realistic and goal oriented. Progress needs to be measurable and monitored during treatment. Typically clients with emotional disorders feel a sense of powerlessness, helplessness and isolation. These feelings need to be carefully addressed. In the following case, Major Depression is highlighted in terms of symptomatology and etiology. Treatment of a chronically depressed client is detailed as well as changes within the therapeutic relationship.

Background - Major Depression

The DSM IV states that Major Depression is an episode of a two week duration or more, which includes at least five critical symptoms of depression. These include depressed mood, some level of anhedonia, significant weight loss or gain, insomnia or hypersomnia, psychomotor changes, lethargy, worthless feelings, poor concentration and suicidal ideation. In addition, clients often have complaints of pain and physical illness. Research indicates that recurrent depressive episodes can be separated by years. This occurs in approximately

one third of the Major Depressive cases. Depressive episodes often occur after a severe psychosocial stressor such as the death of a close relative. In terms of genetics it is 1.5 - 3 times more common for clients with first degree relatives who suffered from Major Depression to develop a Depressive disorder (DSM IV, 1994). Depression also has etiologic roots based on negative cognitions, environmental/psychosocial stressors, and biological problems (i.e., neurochemical imbalance).

Treatment Approaches

There are a variety of treatment approaches that have been used to treat Major Depression. These include: Medication, Electroconvulsive therapy and numerous psychotherapy approaches. Drug efficacy is fairly consistent for three categories of medications. These are Tricyclics (e.g., Tofranil, Elavil), Monoamine Oxidase Inhibitors (e.g., Nardil, Parnate) and Selective Serotonin Reuptake Inhibitors (e.g., Prozac, Zoloft, Paxil). An extensive review of 217 studies states that the average rate of improvement using any of these drugs is 50% (Barlow & Durand, 1995).

Electroconvulsive therapy has been used to dramatically alter brain chemistry in severely depressed patients. It is often used when psychopharmacological approaches yield little results. Currently, it is not clearly understood why ECT is effective. The electroconvulsive shock produces seizure activity which somehow causes depression to decrease.

Cognitive therapy is used extensively to treat depression. In this approach clients are helped to gain insight about their negative cognitions and how this influences their moods. Clients are also encouraged to make logs or journals about their thoughts to discover triggers which may influence their thinking (Barlow & Durand, 1995). One criticism of this therapy strategy is that clients need to be well motivated and capable of focusing on their thinking process.

Combining both medication and psychotherapy is usually recommended. Studies by Hollon et al (1992) and Evans et al (1992) report low relapse rates (15%) for combined treatments compared to medication only (32%) or cognitive therapy only (21%) (cited in Barlow & Durand, 1995) Other therapeutic approaches include supportive, psycho- dynamic, family and brief/task oriented therapies.

Case Presentation

Al is an intelligent verbal male, age 44, with a history of recurrent Major Depression over the past 22 years. The emotional disorder began during his second year in college. His psychiatric admission at that time was one of many consequential interruptions in his life. Al's college studies faltered and he left school without a degree. He experimented with drugs such as LSD, marijuana and hallucinogens, in the 60s and 70s with his "Hippie friends." His feelings fluctuated, from depression due to the death of his father (who also suffered from dysphoria), to elation because of the excitement of the free spirit he

discovered in the Hippie communities. It was, at times, "heaven on earth" with his liberated friends. Traveling across the country, Al was socially active and developed various intimate relationships with women.

Later, the depression immobilized him so that he lost almost all energy, motivation and expression. Auditory hallucinations developed and he was hospitalized for 3 - 9 months nearly every 4 years. Psychiatrists treated him with over 125 Electroconvulsive shocks that resulted in his suffering from memory loss. Al was prescribed a wide selection of medications including antipsychotics, antidepressants and antianxiety agents. During his periods of remission he attended day programs, outpatient psychotherapy, medication monitoring and had various volunteer positions.

His major source of strength came from his supportive mother. She caringly visited him each time he was hospitalized and encouraged him to overcome his mental illness. Al would live with her after discharge. He developed an enmeshed relationship with her and began to obsess about her possible death as she aged. She showed no apparent signs of poor health. Al felt so needy that he could not imagine life without her.

During his periods of partial recovery, Al felt intensely frustrated due to his compulsive hair combing, ordering and checking activities which took up to 2 - 3 hours each night. He seemed to use these compulsive activities to ward off the severe depression in a superstitious manner. Al felt the need to fill his time with these activities. He had a rigid daily schedule which included many hours

of TV watching from 10 p.m. to 4 a.m. Wakeup was at 1 p.m. Furthermore, his problems were compounded due to his obsessive focus on somatic problems such as pains in his ears, teeth, feet and chest.

Due to his intelligence Al was clearly aware of his lost potential and felt deeply angry about this. He expressed bitter jealousy towards the outside world and those who have careers, marriages and finances to do as they please. Sexually frustrated, yet fearful of AIDS, Al felt incapable of developing a romantic relationship. He verbalized his fear of rejection, his fear of change and his fear of depression. In essence, Al walked on eggshells wondering and fearing if his next severe depressive episode was about to begin. As his depression continued, he assumed an illness identity and felt disillusioned due to the doctor's inability to cure him completely.

The client attended weekly psychotherapy sessions and usually ventilated intensely about his frustrations, fears and reactions to daily stressors. Al was hypersensitive in terms of his interactions with others. For example, if the therapist began the session 5 or 10 minutes late he would express anger and frustration about his wait, even though he came 10 to 15 minutes late for his appointments almost every week. He was confronted about his double standard but usually overlooked his faults. Al also exhibited grandiosity in that he described his depression as one of the worst possible cases. His suffering made him unique and was essentially a form of masochistic pride.

Sessions were difficult because the client was highly resistant to suggestions. Due to his fear of change and fear of rejection, he felt unable to seek work, social or educational opportunities. He clung to irrational assumptions, such as his belief that since he has no career, no one would want to socialize with him. We explored how his unemployed status limits his social potential but does not necessarily end it.

The dynamics within the client - therapist relationship were clear. As he expressed the desire to change, and the clinician offered ways to change, he would exhibit resistance to change. The client was essentially self defeating in character. Therefore, the therapeutic tactic was altered and the choice to change was given to the client to decide on his own, when he felt ready. This took pressure off the therapist and clarified how the change potential rests in his hands. Al was encouraged to objectively view his life. He was asked, "What accomplishments do you hope to look back on in your life five or ten years from now?" This was a powerful question to motivate him to think about what he wants to do with his life.

On the one hand, he felt that he has the right to feel negative and angry because he suffered from severe depression for so many years. Al was focusing on playing it safe, in a sense, by doing nothing and not "causing" his depression to redevelop. However, this position was intolerable because of his strong desire to socialize or do something productive. He felt anger toward himself, his

previous doctors and therapists and with this clinician as well. Al desperately wanted someone to solve his problems.

A small group of men were enlisted into group therapy and Al agreed to join. The group offered him a place to socialize and gave him a larger audience to vent his emotional pain and fears. He also began to express some humor as he observed and emulated another group member who used humor as a coping mechanism. The clinician encouraged the use of jokes as a way to release tension. Al developed bonds with the three other group members and they began to socialize after the group by going to a donut shop. Even though Al expressed negative thoughts about his life, he did feel somewhat changed due to these social contacts. When directly challenged, he would admit reluctantly that there are some positive aspects to his life.

His deep desire to develop a romantic relationship would drive him to seek new social connections several times a year. Al joined another group therapy program where he could possibly meet someone. The original men's group encouraged him to do this. He did develop some friendships in the other group, but gave up on them when they showed little interest in him. These setbacks were obsessed about for many weeks.

Continuing in the Men's Group seemed beneficial. Al was compelled to view others problems instead of narcissistically focusing on himself and he did reveal an empathic side which was not apparent before. He also received positive feedback when he told jokes and this encouraged him to continue to do so.

After several months of positive changes, this therapist gave Al a certificate of improvement to highlight and recognize important changes he made. White and Epston (1990) have creatively used certificates to help clients recognize their achievements in therapy. In general, documents are very influential in modern society and often symbolize a new status or position. It also suggests that the individual has reached a point of success. Al, who often felt incapable of achieving anything significant, seemed surprised, encouraged and pleased with the certificate.

Certificate of Improvement

This certificate is granted to Al in recognition of his improvements. This involves his expression of humor and his increased ability in taking more risks socially. He has displayed much effort in the face of considerable adversity. He deserves credit and recognition for these important changes.

As weekly group therapy continued the client was seen individually every three weeks to explore any thoughts or feelings about the group process. At times he was hypercritical about the group members. Nevertheless, he felt strongly connected to them and rarely missed a session.

During treatment, the social worker initially felt angry and impatient with this client. However, by shifting the therapeutic strategy the countertransference also changed from negative to positive. Turner clarifies that "frustration or impatience are frequently perceived by the patient as rejection or loss of control on the part of the caseworker" (Turner, 1983, p.170). Self awareness and control over one's feelings can lead to success with chronic resistant clients. Negative countertransference and blaming the client for therapeutic limitations can hinder the possible success of this type of case.

After four years of treatment, the most dramatic change was exhibited by Al when he came to group and invited the members to go to a Rock concert with him. He took a leadership role and expressed much enthusiasm about the idea. Al even sang some of the songs from the Allman Brothers Band to develop interest in the group. They quickly agreed to go and he purchased the tickets. Al was complimented on his initiative and leadership ability. Approximately two months before this event the therapist had suggested that he do something related to his love of rock music. Apparently he liked the idea but needed time to motivate himself.

In addition, Al continued to complain periodically about his pent up anger and depression but felt a sense of success because he did not need to be psychiatrically hospitalized for the last six years. This was his longest period of staying out of the hospital over the past twenty years.

Conclusion

Many clients ventilate intensely about their emotional struggles and need ongoing therapy and medication to stabilize their emotions. Clinicians often feel pressured to try and "fix problems" by offering advice and encouragement. Some clients are mainly concerned with venting and will resist direct suggestions. They seek emotional support but will not take steps to change. At times their inactivity will be a catalyst to push them to grow. They may feel so bored after a long period that they will have to begin something new and push past their fears. Social workers need to start where the client is at and patiently work with them until these changes can evolve. In addition, group therapy can be productively used to engage, challenge and teach clients new ways to view themselves and to develop coping skills and ego strengths.

In sum, the clinical approach in this case included validation of ongoing progress, reduction of social and emotional isolation, empowering the client, and clarification of small yet realistic goals. This, in turn, led to greater stabilization of his affect and to the development of his life skills, such as initiative and use of humor, as a coping mechanism.

Questions and Answers

Q- Should a therapist keep pictures of his or her family on his desk or wall and would this encourage patients to ask personal questions?

The answer partly depends on the type of clinician. If the therapist wants to maintain firm boundaries and is employing the psychoanalytic or psychodynamic approach to treatment they may prefer not to have any pictures. However many therapists do display family photos and can still conduct treatment effectively. These clinicians usually are doing family therapy, cognitive-behavioral or solution focused therapy. They should still maintain professional boundaries and take care when patients ask personal questions. Many patients feel more connected when they know that they have a family or spouse. The client often believes that the therapist has experience or understanding about relationships. In some cases, though, the patient may feel jealous or even angry that the clinician is married or has children.

Q- Is it acceptable to extend or shorten the length of time of a session?

Mental health professionals often adjust their sessions to match the patient's needs. Severely mentally ill patients who have schizophrenia, bipolar disorder, substance abuse, etc may not have the discipline to converse for more than 20

or 30 minutes. Other clients who are dealing with bereavement, separation or divorce, medical problems, or significant family changes (a child with a terminal illness) may need extra long sessions to cover all the issues and to provide emotional support. I believe that clinicians develop intuition about their patient's needs and can adjust the sessions when needed. These issues can also be addressed in supervision meetings. Therapists should monitor themselves to be sure they don't shorten sessions for clients they dislike and lengthen those for the ones they like.

Q- Is it possible to use the Family Therapy perspective with an individual in treatment?

Certainly the family therapy approach can be used with individuals. The client can be asked many leading questions to help them explore their family relationships and interactions. Many patients who alter the way they interact and communicate with their spouse or family find that they improve emotionally and behaviorally. This certainly relates to the client in the context of their situation.

Q- If a patient asks for direct advice about something they need to do how should this be handled?

In general, it is best to encourage the patient to be independent and shows you respect their judgment when you leave it to them to make decisions. However, some patients may benefit from the clinicians offer to evaluate various choices in a collaborative manner. This is also a form of role modeling and shows them how to assess choices. Showing the client the pros and cons of their possible choices is usually helpful.

Q- Should the clinician tell the patient their diagnosis?

Some therapists are trained to tell their patients about the diagnosis and others not to tell. I would estimate that about half of the patients already know their diagnosis. They may not know the exact name of their disorder but they know they have anxiety, depression, dissociative traits, mood swings, hallucinations, etc. One of the advantages of telling them is that they will gain some clarity about the problem. They may also learn how certain symptoms are linked together to make up the disorder. However, revealing the diagnosis can have negative consequences. Some clients may feel more depressed or even hopeless if they are told they have a serious mental illness. In my practice, I do not reveal the diagnosis to avoid this possibility. If the patient already knows their diagnosis I am more open to discuss the details or symptoms that are involved.

Q- Many patients attend the first or second session and then start canceling or missing appointments. How can this be handled professionally?

An old saying comes to mind: Actions speak louder than words. Why does the client keep saying he/she wants help, but they don't show for their appointments? We need to gently confront the patients about this issue. Do they feel anxious or shameful revealing their personal problems? If so, can we do anything to make it easier for them? Are they aware that most people have some of these feelings? Some patients benefit when the clinician sets firm limits and tells them that the treatment will be terminated if they don't keep their appointments. This should be said without anger or ridicule. Some patients are not ready to commit to ongoing therapy and come for quick crisis intervention. Once the therapist realizes this, they can accept the limited number of sessions. Many clients do not fit into the weekly treatment session that is made consistently for 6 to 12 months. Some patients benefit from biweekly or monthly sessions. I believe it is important to ask the patient how often they want to meet. Let's work around their schedule, if possible, and the chances that they participate and show for appointments may be better.

Q- Is it helpful to ask patients to bring in their artwork, photos, poems or sculptures?

Clients who describe their artwork or photography often have strong feelings about their work. I find it very helpful to see their work and ask them to describe how they feel creating the art and what it means to them. Often this gives me a better under- standing about their creative side and a deeper comprehension of who they are. Some of the clients also struggle with their creative energy. They may find themselves loosing motivation to do art work or photography and this can be explored in treatment. In general, most of the clients want to produce work and feel better when they are functioning well on a creative level. Some of these clients are professional artists and others are hobby-artists.

Q- If conflict develops between the therapist and client should we transfer the case to a different clinician?

Periodically the client will ask for another clinician or hint about it. This issue needs to be explored carefully in sessions. In many cases, if this issue is resolved the therapy will move to a deeper and more productive level. If the transfer is done without an evaluation of the underlying reasons the same pattern of tension may develop with the next therapist. On the other hand there may be a legitimate reason to make the transfer. Perhaps a personality conflict develops between the therapist and client. For example both may be sarcastic and tend to pick on each other. In some cases, the client has a misconception about the

clinician. One of my female clients asked to change to a different counselor. At first, she didn't explain why and I asked her about her reasons. She explained that she felt a woman therapist would be more of a liberal thinker in terms of women's rights. I challenged her to give me a chance as her therapist and explained that she was making an assumption about my views of women. She was also assuming that a woman therapist would have views similar to her. I pointed out that some women have traditional values and may have less interest in women's rights than I do. She accepted this and we continued the sessions.

Q- What can I do to protect myself when I feel intimidated or fearful of a patient?

First, it is important to point out that all cases need to be carefully screened prior to treatment. Is the case appropriate for the clinician and the facility? Perhaps they need to be referred to a more secure clinic or hospital setting. If you are already working with the patient and they raise their voice, the clinician should set limits by asking them to control themselves and reminding them that it is not acceptable. You can also warn them that you or you coworkers will call security if it is necessary. Keeping your office door partly open and sitting near the door are other techniques to give you a sense of safety. Some facilities install panic buttons that set off an alarm in the offices. In some cases, you may need to

transfer the case to another counselor who is more comfortable working with this type of client.

Q- Can the clinician plan a short number of sessions if the client's problems seem minor?

Brief therapy can be offered to many clients who have minor problems. These include making decisions about their social life or career choices. Depending on the setting you may have many other clients with more urgent or severe disorders and may need to prioritize which clients, and for how long, you can treat them. Establishing a number of sessions (perhaps five meetings) as a plan of treatment can help focus the clinical work and keep it moving in the right direction also.

Q- Should the social worker compliment the client when they do something well or succeed with their plans?

Clinicians usually feel excited and proud of their client's accomplishments and often want to give them praise. I believe in most cases it is better to ask the patient how they feel about their success and encourage them to give themselves compliments and praise. In this way they are learning to encourage themselves. Many clients have difficulty doing this. If we are the ones praising

them they may not learn how to do this. In addition, we will not always be available in the future and they need to develop this skill of self praise on their own. At times I will give them compliments but only after they have done so.

Q- What skills can we help our clients develop that they can use in the future after treatment ends?

Depending on the client my goals are to help them improve problem solving skills, self confidence, and trust in their own abilities and decision making. On the cognitive level I hope they will learn to monitor and counter negative thinking patterns. For emotional clients the goal is to help them cope with their affective disorder and learn how to function at their highest level. Many clients also need to learn how to make decisions based on reasoning rather than feelings.

Q- In what ways can we help a Borderline Personality patient stabilize their life?

One of the critical issues for the Borderline is to help them learn how to self soothe. This is essentially learning how to calm themselves down when they become angry, depressed, hopeless or filled with guilt or shame. They also need to understand how their emotional pain often leads to acting out behavior such

as gambling, promiscuity, fights, substance abuse or suicidal gestures. These behaviors are used to cope with their inner pain and are certainly dysfunctional.

Q- What are the key issues when dealing with substance abusers?

Many substance abusers have guilt and shame about their past behavior. They also tend to view themselves negatively. The clients need help to reassess themselves and develop motivation to maintain sobriety. These clients then need to learn what triggers lead to substance abuse and the connection between their cognitions, emotions and behaviors. Many of these clients can be successful when they realize that if they want to change they have to make the decision to improve and work hard at it.

Q- Can the clinician recommend to the client to explore their spiritual side?

Certainly many therapists encourage their clients to attend religious services and events and it seems to positively affect them. The clients realize that they have God as a partner when they face their many life struggles. This helps bolster their resolve to reach goals and gives them additional emotional strength. In some cases, clients also discover a religious community at their church, synagogue or mosque who offer support and friendship. They can benefit on a human and spiritual level as they expand their religious involvement.

Q- Are treatment plans useful?

Treatment plans can be very useful to keep the treatment focused on the goals. When the goals are clear and kept in mind, the sessions won't drift off track. After five or ten sessions the goals should be reevaluated. If the goals have been met new goals can be set up or termination can be considered. In most cases, treatment plans are beneficial especially when they are measurable and observable. An example is to reduce panic attacks to less than 3 times per week and increase sleep to 8 hours per night.

Q- What are the critical questions to ask patients who have suicidal thoughts?

Patients with suicidal thoughts should be asked why they are thinking of suicide. In addition, do they have a plan to kill themselves? Do they have access to a weapon? Are there any reasons that prevent them from committing suicide? Perhaps they have children or religious reasons. It is important to ask if they have any hope for the future. Feeling hopeless is strongly correlated with high suicidal potential. Clients who appear to be at risk should be evaluated by a physician or psychiatrist immediately. If none are available they can be brought to a hospital emergency room for an evaluation.

Q- Should the social worker have a session or intake with a client who is intoxicated on alcohol or drugs?

If it is clear that the patient is intoxicated then the session should be cancelled and rescheduled. I usually tell the patient that they must be sober when they come for appointments. Conducting sessions with patients who are "high" has no value. In most cases, they will be difficult to communicate with and won't remember the session afterward. Furthermore, one should be sure that they have a safe way to get home. The clinician could be liable if they allow the patient to drive home while intoxicated and an accident resulted.

Q- What are the advantages of using group therapy?

Group therapy is useful for clients who are socially isolated and need to develop social skills. Depressed, anxious, psychotic and some personality disordered patients benefit from group therapy. Groups provide emotional support and members often give each other suggestions and ideas. They also act as role models for each other. Often one or more clients are more advanced and can explain how they achieved their accomplishments to the others. Many patients will listen and emulate these fellow patients who have the same disorder and

know how they feel and experience life. Some patients also report that they find Individual therapy too intense. They feel too much focus is on them.

Q- Is it helpful to explain causal factors related to depression or anxiety to the clients?

Educating the patients about their mental health problems is an essential ingredient in clinical work. The clients often feel relieved when they learn that their depression may be due to a chemical imbalance that is treatable. Many of them were blaming themselves for the disorder and trying to "snap out of it." In collaboration with the clinician, the client can clarify if they think their emotional problem is due to stressors, negative cognitions, a chemical imbalance, or a recent crisis. Clarity and insight is the heart and soul of treatment.

Q- How should a therapist handle a patient who describes himself as paranoid, delusional, obsessive, or compulsive?

The clinician needs to ask the client to explain in detail the terms he uses. What does he mean by paranoid? Are both of you using the same definition? In many cases I have found that the clients have incorrect definitions of the

psychological terms he/she uses. Here we can be helpful in clarifying the terms and helping them define their presenting problems accurately.

Q- What can social workers and counselors do to handle feelings of burnout?

Therapists need to take good care of themselves. The work they do can be draining emotionally. Hobbies, vacations, exercise, and outside readings are all good antidotes to burnout. In addition, learning new treatment approaches can be exciting and stimulate new interest in the field. Turning to a helpful supervisor may also prove useful to ask for advice and support when feeling burnout.

Conclusion

This manual reviewed some of the most popular and effective treatment models and their advantages and disadvantages. A number of successful clinical cases were also presented. Clinicians need to develop a strong theoretical foundation which should guide them in their use of interventions and techniques. Clients come for help due to many problems. Many are reacting to crisis events such as a recent assault, an accidental death of a close relative, or a marital breakup. Others are looking inward and trying to understand and cope with auditory hallucinations or overwhelming guilt, shame or depression. During the therapeutic process it is important to create a new experience for the client. The interchange between the therapist and patient needs to explore new perspectives on the presenting problem and should help the client comprehend their self, family, and community. Providing a meaningful therapeutic conversation can have a major impact on them. This, as well as emotional support, is the heart and soul of the treatment. Many patients feel isolated and misunderstood. Their families often don't have the time or resources to help them as much as needed. It is the clinician's role to be available, empathic, and accepting. The ability to create this type of warm and respectful relationship is the basis of good therapeutic work.

It is critical to add a caveat to the various cases which have been presented. Clinicians should not assume that their clients have all the same characteristics

and family dynamics as the cases presented here. Therefore, the interventions may not fit well for others. Therapists should rather consult their supervisors about their particular cases and explore intervention options. Some of my interventions may apply but should be used after careful consideration and under guidance. It is my hope that this manual will benefit professionals in the mental health field and will provide some understanding of clinical treatment possibilities.

BIBLIOGRAPHY

American Psychiatric Association (1994) Diagnostic and Statistical Manual of Mental Disorders, Fourth Edition, Washington, DC, American Psychiatric Association.

Barlow, D. And Durand, M. (1995) Abnormal Psychology: An Integrative Approach, Ca: Brooks/Cole.

Dorfman, R. (1988) Paradigms of Clinical Practice, NY: Brunner / Mazel.

Gurman, A. and Kniskern, D. (1981) Handbook of Family Therapy, NY: Brunner / Mazel.

Hudson – O'Hanlon, W. (1989) In Search of Solutions, NY: W.W.Norton.

Safran, J. and Muran, J. (2000) Negotiating the Therapeutic Alliance, NY: Guilford.

Turner, F. (1983) Differential Diagnosis and Treatment in Social Work, NY: The Free Press.

Turner, F. (1996) Social Work Treatment, NY: The Free Press.

White, M. and Epston, D. (1990) Narrative Means to Therapeutic Ends. NY: Norton.